Baby Farm Animals

Baby Pigs

By Nick Rebman

level
1
little blue
readers

Little Blue House is distributed by North Star Editions:
sales@northstareditions.com | 888-417-0195

Produced for Little Blue House by Red Line Editorial.

Photographs ©: Shutterstock Images, cover, 4, 7, 9, 11, 12–13, 14, 17, 18–19, 20, 23, 24 (top left), 24 (top right), 24 (bottom left), 24 (bottom right)

Library of Congress Control Number: 2021916725

ISBN
978-1-64619-478-0 (hardcover)
978-1-64619-505-3 (paperback)
978-1-64619-558-9 (ebook pdf)
978-1-64619-532-9 (hosted ebook)

Printed in the United States of America
Mankato, MN
012022

About the Author

Nick Rebman is a writer and editor who lives in Minnesota. He enjoys reading, drawing, and taking long walks with his dog.

Table of Contents

Baby Pigs

I see baby pigs.

They sleep in the straw.

A baby pig stands up.

It is very small.

The baby pig has a big nose.

It also has big ears.

The baby pigs go outside.
They stay near
their mother.

The baby pigs walk in the mud. The mud helps them stay cool.

Eating and Drinking

The baby pigs need food.

They get milk from

their mother.

Soon the baby pigs eat solid food.

They eat a mix of corn, wheat, and more.

It is called feed.

feed

The baby pigs drink water.

It comes from a pipe.

Growing Up

The baby pigs stay together.

They live in a group.

The baby pigs start to grow up.
Soon they will have their own babies.

Glossary

feed

pipe

mud

straw

Index

24